By **Dot Meharry**
Illustrated by **Meredith Thomas**

Contents

Chapter 1 At the Brickworks

John's dad had a new job. Early in the mornings, Dad would take his truck and pick up a load of clay. Then he would take the load to the brickworks in the city.

John sat in the truck beside Dad. It was the holidays, so John went with him.

The sun was just coming up as they drove over the hills.

Dad told John all about the tall chimneys at the brickworks. He talked about the big shed where he dumped the clay. He talked about how the clay was used to make bricks. He told John about the pigeons that made nests in the sheds.

John liked birds. He had two hens at home called Took-Took and Chooky. Every day, he went to the hen house to get their eggs and clean the straw. He couldn't wait to see the pigeons at the brickworks.

The truck climbed slowly up the last hill then went down to the city. The load of clay was heavy.

"Can you see the chimney tops?" asked Dad. He pointed to them. John thought they looked like giant needles.

Dad talked about how the bricks were made from the clay.

"They have to be put in big ovens," said Dad.

But John wished Dad would talk more about the pigeons.

That morning, a hungry cat was near the shed at the brickworks. The cat knew that sometimes baby birds fell out of their nests. It looked up at the birds in their nests.

Suddenly, something dropped down! The cat crept towards the bundle of feathers on the ground. It was just about to pounce when Dad and John drove into the shed.

The noisy truck scared the cat. It ran out of the shed.

"Did you see that cat?" cried John. "Maybe it was looking for a bird to eat."

The truck stopped. The brakes hissed and frightened some of the pigeons. They flew out of the shed and far away.

Chapter 2 Pidge

John had to stay in the truck. Dad wanted to make sure he was safe.

John looked in the mirror next to his window. He could see the truck's tray begin to rise. Up and up it went.

Then, John saw something move on the ground.

"Stop, Dad!" he shouted. "There's something behind the truck."

Dad stopped the tray, just as the clay was about to slide off.

"It looks like a bird flapping around," cried John. "I bet that's what the cat was after."

"We'd better check before we dump the clay," said Dad. He lowered the tray back down. Then they climbed out of the truck to have a look.

A baby bird flapped her little wings. She was trying to fly away. But her body was too heavy. Her wings were just too little. John sat beside the frightened pigeon.

"She must have fallen from her nest," John said, looking up at the nests. "Can we take her home with us? That cat will come back and get her if we don't."

“All right, we’ll take her home,” Dad said. “But let’s dump this load of clay first. We need to get out of here before another bird falls from a nest! You already have Took-Took and Chooky.”

John put his hands under the bird. He lifted her up. Dad saw how gentle he was with the little pigeon.

John climbed back into the truck. He held the little pigeon in his hands. The pigeon was shaking. John knew how scared she must be, with all the strange smells and sounds around her.

He gently patted the bird. She still had soft baby feathers. John wondered how she had fallen out of the nest. He wondered if her parents would miss her.

As the truck drove towards home, John thought about what he could feed the little bird. His chickens, Took-Took and Chooky, ate mashed corn. John didn't know what pigeons ate. He would have to find out.

"Why don't you give the bird a name?" said Dad.

"Mmmm," said John. "Pidge! That's short for pigeon!"

Chapter 3

Aunty Sue to the Rescue

Back home, John put some straw from Chooky's nest inside a box. He made it look like a real nest. He put Pidge in it.

Next, he mixed some of the hens' mash with water. He put the food in front of Pidge and waited for her to eat. Pidge sat and sat. She didn't even open her eyes to look at the food.

John put some mash on his fingers. He pressed Pidge's beak into it, but she kept her beak shut. Again and again, John tried to get the pigeon to eat. He knew the little bird *had* to eat and drink. She was already thirsty and weak.

"You've done your best," said John's mum quietly. "There's nothing more you can do."

John was upset. He'd saved Pidge from the cat. Then, he had an idea. They could take Pidge to Aunty Sue. She was a vet. She could help.

Mum, Dad and John got into the car. This was an emergency!

"WEEE-ooo, WEEE-ooo," sang Dad. "Make way for the bird ambulance!"

He was trying to make John laugh, but it didn't work. John was too worried about Pidge.

At the vet clinic, Aunty Sue looked at the little bird. John told her how he had tried to get Pidge to eat mash like Took-Took and Chooky.

"Pigeons don't eat the way hens do. They use their beaks like a straw," she said. "They poke their beaks into their parents' beaks and sip pigeon milk."

Now John understood why Pidge would not eat or drink.

"I can give you a special bird feeder and some baby bird food," she told him.

John was happy. Pidge was going to be all right now!

Back home, John put some of the bird food in the feeder. He tried to open Pidge's beak to get the feeder inside her mouth. Pidge would not open her beak. She just sat and sat. John felt sick. How could he save Pidge now?

Chapter 4

Surprise

At bedtime, John took Pidge to his room and shut the door. He sat on his bed. Tears filled his eyes. He wished he'd left Pidge at the brickworks. Maybe the cat wouldn't have come back. Maybe Pidge would have made it back into her nest somehow.

The next morning, John didn't get up early as he usually did.

"I hope Pidge is okay," said Mum to Dad.

"John will be so upset if she's not," said Dad.

At last, John came out with the box. Mum put her arms around him.

"It's all right, John," she said. "You did your best to save Pidge."

His parents looked in the box.

"I tried to save Pidge—and I did! Surprise!" shouted John. He laughed with joy.

Pidge looked up at Mum and Dad. "*Peep*," she went in her pigeon voice. She was alive and well.

"How did you save her?" asked Mum and Dad.

John held up an old T-shirt.

"Watch this," he said.

John put some wet bird food close to a small hole he'd made in the T-shirt. He pulled the cloth around some food. Then he squeezed it into a ball. Some of the food oozed through the hole.

Pidge poked her beak into the hole. She sipped up the wet food wrapped in the T-shirt. She used her beak like a straw.

Mum and Dad were amazed. John had found a way to feed Pidge!

Pidge snuggled down into the nest in the box. She tucked her little head under her wing. She was soon fast asleep.

"You're a good dad, John," said Dad.

Everyone laughed. John was so happy that he had saved Pidge. When she could fly, he would take her back to the shed at the brickworks. She belonged with her pigeon family.